MW01135481

Don't Rush Me:

Selected Poems of Dwain
Preston

Don't Rush Me: Selected Poems of Dwain Preston

Copyright © 2016 by Dwain Preston

All rights reserved. This book or any portion thereof may not be reproduced or used in any manner whatsoever without the express written permission of the publisher except for the use of brief quotations in a book review or scholarly journal.

First Printing: 2016

ISBN 978-1-329-82875-9

Red Flyer Wagon Publishing
Quincy IL 62301

Don't Rush Me:

Selected Poems of Dwain Preston

To Regina

A Brief History of Dwain

Dallas Dwain Preston was born near Barry, Illinois on February 21st, 1936, the first child of Nellie and Claude Preston. They would go on to have four more children after Dallas—Ronald, Lewis, Nadine and Donna. Oh, and nobody ever called him Dallas. He was Dwain from the beginning.

The first years of Dwain's life were spent in a tiny house close to Barry, but in 1944, the family moved to the "big" city of Quincy. They lived in the Indian Hills Projects until 1947 and Dwain went to Berrian School on South 8th Street. Then, it was back to another farm—this one, in Richfield Township. Dwain would attend four different one-room schools in Pike and Adams counties before finally graduating from Liberty Community Unit #3 High School in 1953.

After high school, Dwain went to Western Illinois State Teachers College (now Western Illinois University) in Macomb, where he received his Bachelor's Degree in 1957. He enlisted in the Air Force and was sent to Yale Language School. He served as a Chinese Language Specialist, was stationed in Texas and eventually in Taiwan (he'd know it as Formosa). Following the service, Dwain returned once again to Illinois.

Dwain's first job as a teacher was at Quincy Junior High School. He was hired in 1961 and stayed until 1967, mostly in the history department. His own history, however, would be changed forever when friends introduced him to a young woman named Regina Ann Higgins. The story goes that this Catholic girl had been praying novenas to find a husband, so maybe someone was looking out for her when she met Dwain. They were married in May of 1962, and between 1963 and 1966 they had four girls: Carolyn, Cheri, Debbie and Teresa.

Dwain got his Master's Degree from W.I.U. and his PhD from the University of Illinois in Champaign. The family settled in Macomb, where Dwain (now a professor) was a member of the English Faculty at Western Illinois University. He taught there until 1978. The next year, Dwain found out that good teachers and great poets make lousy salesmen. The family moved back to Quincy and Dwain tried his hand at selling insurance, which was, in his own words, a miserable failure.

Where else to go but back to the classroom? This time, Quincy Notre Dame came calling. Dwain gave up the university professorship and decided to teach high school. It was, he would say, the smartest decision he ever made, besides marrying Regina. For more than 25 years, QND was his home. He earned the nickname "Doc" and the respect of thousands of students. He taught Speech and English, moderated the student council, chaperoned school trips, drove a bus, and was a mentor to many, many young people throughout his career. For several years, Regina worked at Notre Dame in the Development Office, and most mornings they drove to and from school together, talking about the day, or the latest on what was happening with their girls.

Just a few weeks after Dwain retired in 2006, Regina passed away. Since then, Dwain has taught at John Wood Community College, become a professional story-teller, been welcomed as a member of the Quincy Public Library Board, taken part in Quincy Community Theater, and continued to teach as a substitute.

Introduction

       Carolyn, Debbie, Teresa and I have a game we play when we come home to Quincy. We try to guess how many people Dad will say "hi" to on a trip to the grocery store, church, or out to breakfast. It's usually between 10 and 50, but we have a long-standing debate over whether couples count as one "hi" or two. Those trips often stretch out over several hours, because Dad, quite simply, knows most everyone in town.

       These poems represent Dad's life, and are divided into four sections. First: Growing up on the Farm. Reading them, it becomes clear how much those one-room schoolhouses and Illinois plow-fields meant to him. There's "Kate and Nell," who were to be replaced, eventually, by modern machinery and "That Little Ole Brown Buildin," which was to be replaced by indoor plumbing. "Going to Get the Mail" is a look back on days when sumacs swayed and sighed and when a trip to the mailbox included a glass of iced tea with the neighbors. One of my favorites, "A Matter of Distance," is the story of a young man from the city's first encounter with "cuttin' hogs."

       The second section is called "Nature," and it shows Dad's deep love for the outdoors. "God Speaks to the June Wildflowers" is the result of traveling back and forth across Western Illinois for several years. "Mea Culpa" goes out to anyone who's ever killed a living thing that's run across the road in front of your car and "November Twilight" is a farewell to the day. I like to read this one and imagine looking out over the Mississippi River as the sun sets on a late Autumn evening.

The third section is called "Life." This is where the family comes in. Dad wrote a poem for each of us on our wedding day—and for each of our children on his or her 13th birthday. Those may make another volume. For now, you have "Time, Time, Time," which was written during those hectic days when we were all trying to get to class before the bell rang, and to band practice, sports, jobs and friends' houses after school. Teaching has been a very big part of Dad's life and that is reflected in poems like "The Writing Teacher," about the inadequacies educators sometimes feel and "The Substitute," about giving up daily duties in place of part-time employment. Of course, there are also poems dedicated to Mom. "For Regina" was written after she died and is a tribute to his one true love. The one that reminds me of Mom the most, however, is "Southern Memories," about a road trip they took together to Florida.

Finally, we have "Songs," because Doc Preston is a singer. Always has been. As babies, we were bounced on his knee to the tune of "Bonanza" and as toddlers, he sang us to sleep with "Red River Valley," "Go Tell Aunt Rhody," and "Streets of Loredo" (usually the Smothers Brothers version). Of course Dad is going to make up his own songs! He always said that one of his great regrets in life was not learning to play the guitar. Maybe someone who can will put these to music someday.

The book itself is called "Don't Rush Me" because that poem is about growing older. It's also something Dad says all the time. We love you loads, Dad. Happy 80th Birthday.

Cheri Preston Landis
Carolyn Preston Sloan
Debbie Preston Crowe
Teresa Preston Peavy
February, 2016

FARM

That Little Old Brown Buildin'

It sat off from our country home
About a half a mile
(Or at least it seemed that far to me
When I was still a child!).

It had two holes and catalogues
And cobwebs on the floor—
That little old brown buildin'
With the moon cut in the door!

In the summer time the smell was bad
(Even when we used the lime),
But we had to go when nature called
No matter what the time.

We always yearned for the flushin' kind
But we were kinda poor,
So we hurried down to the buildin' brown
With the moon cut in the door!

I still can feel that winter wind
A-blowin' through the crack;
When I would sit down on the hole
It whistled up my back!

I oft-times think of the family farm,
But I won't go back no more
To that little old brown buildin'
With the moon cut in the door!

Hutchinson, Kansas

The sign speeds by
And quickly stamps its imprint
On my mind: "Hutchinson."
I wonder, do they remember,
1931, my father,
Young and single,
Riding the rails, being picked up here,
By a railroad bull,
And turned over
To the cops?
"Where are you headed?"
They asked.
"I think I'll go downtown
And hit up Sally."
"Like hell," they said,
And took him to the edge
Of town, maybe right there,
By the sign.
"Don't ever come back
To Hutchinson."
And he didn't.
I wonder, do they remember?

Goin' To Get the Mail

When life takes on too fast a pace
And stresses replace joy,
I'd like to sit and think of things
I did when I's a boy.

One "think" that's in my treasure box
Is not for trade or sale:
The memory, so fond to me,
Of goin' to get the mail.

It's always summer in my mind;
The sumacs sway and sigh
As I begin my half-mile walk,
The sun mid-morning high.

I hear the red-winged blackbird call,
The meadow lark and quail,
As down the gravel road I trudge
To get the morning mail.

There where the dusty highways cross
The boxes are arrayed
The neighbor kids are waiting too,
Beneath the elm tree's shade.

We shout hello and then sit down
And look up in the sky,
And guess that it's "'bout 'leven o'clock—
Or just a little shy."

We cross the fence and wade the pond
Or catch a wandering toad,
And then go back to shade our eyes
To look 'way down the road.

There, three stops down, a mile away,
Across the hazy vale,
Is mailman Leo's trusty jeep
A-bringin' us the mail!

We chew on long-stemmed ticklelgrass
And break up clods of clay,
And wonder, and anticipate
What we might get this day—

A package from Montgomery Ward,
A card from Uncle Dale,
Newspapers, bills, and letters too,
Would all be in the mail!

Then he pulls up and hands it out;
I start the long trip back,
With all those precious items
In a paper grocery sack.

I make a stop at Maggie's house;
She's old and kind of frail.
She hoes her little garden patch,
But can't go get the mail.

I drink iced tea and gossip some
(cause Maggie likes to talk!);
I wipe the sweat from off my face
And then I homeward walk.

I read the daily "funnies" then—
"Red Ryder," "Ally Oop"—
and then have lunch—a steaming bowl
of Mom's potato soup.

Some memories just fade away
When life gets kind of stale,
But one that always perks me up
Is "goin' to get the mail!"

Kate and Nell

Just a pair of old plow horses? Yes,
But all my city days have taught me less
Than Kate and Nell, the dappled team of grays
Who shared my work and play of youthful days.

Four decades have not caused me to forget
The earthy air of horse dung, urine, and sweat,
Or taste of dust, or sight of daffodils
As we worked dawn to dusk across those fields.

But we developed fond companionship,
And neither of them felt the stinging whip
Of reins. In turn, they gave me happy hours
Of bareback riding through the woods and flowers.

They taught me how committees work. Old Kate—
Fat, sleek, and wise—would concentrate
On image-building. Nell, her single-tree
Pulled tight, would dig to do the work of three.

With harness, hames, and collars put away,
Fresh curried, they would turn to pasture play.
Detached from labor, they would run
And roll beneath the setting summer sun.

I find it hard to think they were not sad
To be replaced by modern means.
My dad, to render "cost-effective" our old farm,
For "super horsepower" traded love and charm.

I do not know their end. I do recall
The day the stock truck came to haul
Them off. And since that day I do not care
To hear that bouncy song, "The Old Gray Mare."

Boomer

Now Uncle Dan and Auntie Clare
Lived off on a neighboring farm
That I liked to visit 'cause they had sheep,
And sheep have a certain charm.

I got to watch at shearing time,
And see the lambs bein' born,
And once in a while I'd round 'em up
When they all got loose in the corn.

At the head of the flock was Boomer,
A buck who was big and bad,
And when Uncle Dan wasn't lookin',
I'd tease him and make him mad.

I rattled a chain in front of him,
Then away to the gate I sped,
And just as I climbed to the very top board,
He'd slam the gate with his head!

I told my daddy what I had done.
He said, "Don't brag or strut."
Old Boomer's gonna have his day,
He's gonna bang somebody's butt!

And you had better not tell Dan,
Or you won't go no more! "
But I just looked for other ways
To make old Boomer sore.

That summer Cousin Russell came
From St. Louis town to stay
And then, to tease old Boomer
We had a brand new way!

Now Russ had been to the opera house
(of culture he was full!),
and since he'd been to "Carmen" last,
Old Boomer became a bull!

When Russ would wave that big red flag,
That buck was filled with hate!
He'd run, and Russ would pull it back,
And Boomer'd bang the gate!

Well, one day goin' to Uncle
Dan's We came up over the hill,
And saw a sight we'd never seen
(And again we never will):

Somebody'd left that pasture gate
As open as the seven seas,
And there was Boomer going through
As handsome as you please!

Up in the garden was Auntie Clare,
Pickin' beans a-bendin' over,,
And Boomer could see her big red dress
Through the dandelions and clover!

What happened next I won't relate.
Let's say it wasn't nice.
For all of Russ's bandana waves
Aunt Clare would pay the price!

When Uncle Dan and Auntie Clare
Found out what we had done,
Old Boomer was sold and we was spanked
For a long, long summer's fun!

My story's over but Dad was right—
This lesson I'll be leavin':
If you're going to tease a big buck sheep,
Just know—he'll be getting' even!

A Matter of Distance

One Friday night
My college roommate, Joe
Decided he'd come home with me
To see how farm folk live.
The next day, after breakfast,
Dad announced the morning's project:
"Cuttin' hogs."

"Now of exactly what does that comprise?"
Asked Joe,
All eager to assist with country chores.
"Well, Joe, I don't much know
No better way to tell ya, son:
To make the boy-hogs market-fat
We have to cut their balls."

Those boar-pigs didn't like too much
The major surgery that we performed that day.
And neither much, did Joe.

He grimaced when we slammed them down,
Left side against the ground.
And, knees upon their bellies, held them fast,
Front legs across the back.
He turned away as Dad began
The quick, incisive cuts, each side the seam,
And pulled the organs from
Their life-producing source.

And as their shrill and bootless squeals
Sliced through the April air,
We looked—and Joe was gone.

He missed the final "humane" touch—
The healing salve of turpentine and lard.
And as each new-made barrow ran away

To soothe his savaged pride,
We would begin again—
But not with Joe.

The Rocky Mountain Oyster fete
That we had planned that night
Was carried out without the honored guest.
Joe had to hurry back
To school
"to study for an early Monday quiz."

The rest of that semester
Joe would hardly ever speak to me
Except to say
He thought country folks were cruel.
Commencement came; we parted ways.

Some years had passed when I saw Joe again,
Our rendezvous a famous fast-food place.
A lawyer now, he advocates
The rights of animals.
And as he outlined his new thing,
The "Anti-Hog Confinement" cause
He nibbled on a sandwich made of ham.

Why Nobody Calls Me "Handyman"

Don't hand me no wrenches or buckets of paint,
"Cause a fix-it man I surely ain't!
Now I got a brother who can take a barn
And build it into a house, by darn!

He can tune an engine or frame a door--
When one job's done, he's ready for more!
That kind of talent didn't come to me--
I found out early, don't you see,

When I was about thirteen or so.
My dad said, "Son, it's time you know
How to handle tools and do repairs
On busted gaskets and creakin' stairs.

Your younger brother has already learned
How to handle wires and not get burned,
How to sharpen a hoe, and pound a nail,
And tie a knot that'll never fail.

So get the tool box outta the shed,
And fix that hay rack wagon bed.
And that Ford tractor's had a fit.
So see what you can do with it.

And try to have it done real soon.
We're gonna haul hay this afternoon."
Well, I went to the barn with trepidation
(This wasn't gonna be a beach vacation!).

The wagon floor was a little sick
(Had a hole the size of Lonesome Crick!),
The boards were wobbly, a tire half flat--
But I knew how to take care of that.

With some baling wire and a tire pump,
She was ready to move, she was ready to jump!
But then I thought, "Oh, Precious Lord,
What'll I do with the ailin' Ford?" ·

She choked and whined when I turned the key,
And why she died was a mystery.
I unhooked the gasoline line and blew it
('Cause I'd once watched somebody do it!),

And when I gave her another hit,
She purred like a kitten, so I just quit.
I put the tools back in their place,
And went to feed my hungry face.

The high point of the tale I tell
Came on that afternoon from Hell!
Me and my dad and Elmo Clay
Went out to pick up baled hay.

Dad drove the Ford and pulled the wagon,
I sat on the rack with Elmo, braggin'
'Bout how I could fix most anything
With a pair of pliers or a ball of string.

Elmo just wore a troubled smile,
"N after we'd gone about a mile,
He worried aloud about workin' for hire
When he saw the hole and the baling wire!

Pretty soon we started our job for the day
Of picking up bales of clover hay.
Old Elmo was a man with pluck,
And he stacked up high the bales I'd buck.

He was reckoned to be the best around
(The old boys talked of it in town!).
He covered the boards, the hole and the wire.
I kept on buckin', and he stacked 'em higher.

When we started uphill on the road to home,
Those bales were higher than the hills of Rome--
Those bales were higher than anything!
On top sat Elmo--the hay bale king!

I was walkin' along with a big old smirk,
Proud of the load, proud of my work,
When all of a sudden that tractor spit,
And coughed and sputtered and wheezed and quit!

Dad hit the brakes, but it wasn't no use--
By that time Hell had busted loose!
That big old pyramid of clover
Was rollin' fast and leanin' over.

The wagon bed began to shake,
And then I heard the wire break!
The tire I'd pumped went flat as a door
And a bottom bale went through the floor!

(I tell you this in freeze-frame style,
But things were happenin' a minute a mile!)
My dad was cussin'- the air was blue!--
And Elmo was screamin', "What should I do?"

Then everything ended really quick,
When the wagon slammed into Lonesome Crick.
Hay bales went flyin' everywhere!
The tractor sat with it nose in the air.

What I remember--though it wasn't our goal--
Is Elmo and Dad in the swimmin' hole,
Headin' for shore and the hickory tree,
Blubberin' and cussin' and callin' for me!

Over the rest I'll draw the curtain,
But I'll tell you one thing for certain:
Nobody ever asked me again
To tighten a bolt or fix a pen,

And though they call me ever'thing they can,
Nobody calls me "Handyman"!

The Hayhook: A Gift

Remember this old reprobate?
Already dulled and rusted down
From several summers' swinging
In the hayfields, it turned up
On our farm some twenty
Years ago. You nailed it
To the south wall of our
Milking barn. Remember?
All kinds of things hung on it there—
Cow kickers, rope and baseball hats,
Foam-covered twelve-quart pails of milk,
And many dreams.
A year or so ago I wandered back,
Replenishing my need for country things.
This hook was there, still fastened
To the wall. I pried it loose.
Six hundred years of Anglo-Saxon law
Will claim I stole the property
Of someone else, but I don't care.
The memories that hang from this
Are ours. So if you don't mind
Taking pilfered goods, here 'tis.
I wouldn't try the buckets on it now.
But it will hold your hat.
And maybe just a dream or two
If you can push those memories aside
To make them room.

NATURE

Blue Jay

From limb to barren limb
He flits,
A flash of brightened blue
Against a drab November day.
With saucy screech
And balanced, fanning tail
He bends and folds,
Spindles and mutilates
A mind programmed
To ponder somber things.

Blue Heron

Perhaps a yard above the bay,
His head curved back.
The great blue heron
Waves his graceful wings
And glides from cove to cove.
But when he once decides to land,
His toothpick legs protrude,
Broad-jumper style.
And in he comes,
Utility replacing grace,
To make a three-point splash.
He then begins his breakfast walk.
His head and neck
Protruding, then receding,
With each stilt-step stride
Until, wings out,
His head bobs quickly down,
Submerges and returns—
And fish between his bills!

Mea Culpa

Commandeering tons of steel,
I hurtle down the country road
At sixty miles an hour,
With chicory and Queen Anne's lace
Kow-towing in my wake.
My brazenness is equaled by
The birds at feeding time,
As robins, cardinals, grackles, crows,
Strut openly in evening shade,
And seem to taunt
This mechanized intrusion of
A rite as old as life.
Each flock flies up,
As jettisoned,
And 'scapes my mighty wheels.
"I don't know how they do it,
But they do!" I say,
Complacent in my knowledge
Of the ways of birds and men,
When, suddenly, before my eyes,
A mourning dove,
Her vertical ascension
Just a mini-second short,
Gives one last beat of wings.
Her plump and tender body
Thuds against my windshield
And leaps into the air.
The rear-view shows her bounding
In the road, as scattered feathers,
Gray and white, drift slowly to the ground.

A small and meaningless event?
Perhaps. Yet I have found
Siddhartha, Christ nor Shiva
Provide a paradigm
To hold my pain and guilt
At having needlessly destroyed
A small and feathered thing.

God Speaks with the June Wildflowers

One morning God, in a leafy glade,
Sat down to think of the things he'd made.

"Man really makes Me mad sometimes;
he seldom cares for art or rhymes."

There's just so much that he could see—
And if he did, he'd think of Me!"

After He'd thought for many hours,
He called together the Midwest flowers.

"I need some help, and I need it soon—
a color scheme for the month of June.

Those people drive looking straight ahead.
And never to the side," he said.

"So what will make them pause a while,
and think good thoughts, and maybe smile?"

Sweet Chicory was the first to speak:
"I think the color that you seek

Is a gentle blue, and soft and mellow"
Wild Mustard spoke: "Oh no! Bright yellow,

Spread like a carpet, far and wide."
At that, the vetch and clover sighed.

"The rug idea is right out front,
but lavender is the shade you want!"

Milkweed assented, and Thistle too—
They both agreed on the purple hue.

"There's something to be said for brown,"
said Sourdock, who was hooted down.

"Let's make it tan," said tall Rye Grass,
"And through it let the soft wind pass."

"A white would remind them of Your grace."
Said Morning Glory and Queen Anne's Lace.

"Oh yes! Oh yes! Let white take over!"
said Elderberry and tall Sweet Clover.

Parsnips and fleabanes shouted, "Right!
There's nothing as pure as a flower of white!"

Old Trumpet Vine, high on a post,
Said, "A deep dark orange would do the most."

Someone retorted, "Don't be silly:
Let's choose the orange of me—Day Lily!"

Then Sumac spoke. "A deep blood red
Would remind them of Your death," she said.

Daisy, and Mullein, and Cornflower tall
All said that yellow was best of all.

Then God intoned, "That's all today.
You've each had a chance to have your say.

And now I know what I have to do—
I'll spread roadsides with all of you!"

Miniature Oracle

A sleepy summer garden
Holds a cosmos of surprise.
Its impact on a larger world
Only sages may surmise.

Today's epiphany: the breeze
Blows petals to disclose
A simple small white spider
On the sepal of a rose.

Gentle Persuasion

If you had asked me yesterday,
I'd say, and never bend:
A scheme of yellow, black and blue?
There's no way they will blend.

A scene this morning in my yard
Has made me change my story:
I saw a rotund bumblebee
Inside a morning glory.

Gina's Pansies

Beneath the shade of the redbud tree
Gina's pansies dance for me.
Sometimes brazen, sometimes coy,
Their somber looks belie their joy

The summer wind and the morning sun
Entice the grass to join the fun.
Now daisies prance, and zinnias too,
And a red-pink hollyhock or two.

A sparrow revamps his would-be stroll
As he sports about in the birdbath bowl.
A tiny butterfly of white
Flits by on his Thursday flight.

St. Anthony stands among the plants
And tells the Child of the garden dance.
I muse, as I contemplate this bliss:
Gina's pansies started this!

Here's to the Carp

I strike my harp for the lowly carp,
That giant beast of the goldfish clan.
He's the best darn fish to grace the dish
Of woman or of man.

There are those, no doubt, who would vote for trout,
Swordfish, or walleyed pike.
And bass is sharp, but give me carp-
Now there's the fish I like!

Some say carp's crude to eat as food
They blanch when carp come near.
Carp may eat grime and swim in slime—
But God! They're good with beer!

If you throw a line into the brine
With a hook and Wheatie ball,
A carp will bite, and give you a fight
Till you nail him to the wall!

And then filleted, and fried and laid
On a plate with good cole slaw—
Why, you can wish for a big catfish,
But carp? It has no flaw!

So when you call for a vote, just make this note:
Here's mine, and it's my label—
"I strike my harp for the lowly carp,
From the river to the table!"

Bronco Moon

A copper-colored, slim and sleek.
Unbroken-bronco moon
High-rides the western sky tonight.
And, as I travel toward him
Over dipping roadway hills,
He jumps and bucks, sunfishes
Through the silhouettes of trees,
And comes down hard
Upon the horizon.

The Trees of My Life

In western Oklahoma I surveyed
The treeless, soapweed-scattered fields of wheat
And made the Illinoisan's sad lament,
"You need some trees to overcome the heat."

"Oh, you don't understand," my cousin said,
 "We don't care much to travel in your state.
The trees get in the way of all the scenery
And make it hard for us to concentrate."

Get in the way? Get in the way? I thought.
A worldview like this? How could it be
 That one could miss the beauty of a scene
And blame his lack of vision on a tree?

No segment of my life is quite complete
Without the memory of a favorite tree.
They stand in yards and farms and parks,
And each, I think, is some small part of me.

Beside the old frame house where I was born,
Outside the bedroom window stood an ash,
And later, through its limbs I saw the moon,
And felt the wind, and saw the lightning flash.

Much later, as I spent time in the town,
A lonesome, windswept pine became my friend.
It stood atop an ancient Indian mound.
From there I watched the Mississippi bend.

And on the 80-acre boyhood farm
My best companion was a white oak tree.
I told it secrets, climbed its far-flung limbs;
It shared my dreams of what I wished to be.

One night beneath a burly sycamore
I asked my future wife to marry me.
We lived together over forty years;
Our marriage was as sturdy as that tree.

Behind the house where all my children grew
A slender weeping willow graced the sky.
A tire swing hung from a supple limb,
And there my children learned that they could fly.

Today, above where I transcribe these lines
A redbud spreads its canopy of shade.
A quarter century it has housed the birds,
And in its limbs my grandchildren have played.

So if there's nothing there but boundless plain,
Do not extol its beauty, if you please.
My life has taught me always to beware
A landscape that's devoid of any trees.

The Leaves Come Dancing

Today I got a special treat.
> The leaves came dancing down the street.

> This week they had all fallen down—
Red ones, yellow ones, gold ones, brown—
> They lay like carpet, colors bold,
> > Upon the sidewalk where I
> strolled.

> Then, as the wind began to blow,

The leaves put on an autumn show.

> They whirled and made my day complete

As they came dancing down the street.

November Twilight

Sandwiched
Between October's clashing colors
And December's satin snow,
November's Mississippi bluffs
Are bleak and brown and bare.
But Ah! November's twilights;
I search to find the perfect words
To capture, hold and memorize
This one majestic moment:
A bright magenta sunset
Beyond a plodding river.
Kaleidoscopic orange and red
And yellow hues
Form silhouettes
Of naked, round-topped trees.
A barge's after-tow
Disturbs the river's
Glassy, green-brown glaze.
And waves begin
To slip and slap and slosh
Upon the ferry dock
And stone retaining walls.
As blue and purple firmament
Begins to shade to black.
The moving mallards cry,
"Too soon! Too soon!"
Theirs but an echo of
The poignant human plaint:

"Oh day, come back,
And let me live you once again!
The moment quickly passes on,
But I have savored one small gift of God—
A brief November twilight.

LIFE

My Fourth of July Baby

Now Bobbi is my baby
And I'll tell you why:
She's a walkin' talkin'
Fourth of July!
When Bobbi bops
Into a room
The fireworks start—
       Va Voom!
            Va Voom!

Have you ever been
To a 'works display
At the end of a long
Independence Day,
With the boats in the harbor
And the red-orange sky,
And the dark comin' on
Like chocolate pie,
And the cherry bombs startin'
In City Park?
Well Bobbi's got
That kind of spark!
And when Bobbi rolls
Her baby blues
I get a feelin'
In the toes of my shoes

Like those big-bang boomers
That burst and spray
All green and pink
And bright as day.

When Bobbi puts
Her hand in mine
And we get as close
As a quarter to nine,
My heart goes Poof!
      And Tink!
            And Wop!
Like the little firecrackers
That pop!
      Pop!
                  Pop!

The Writing Teacher

"Authority," "surprise," "detail," and "metaphor."
From book to brain to mouth the terms flow out.
And quickly wind up scribbled white on black
Before the fifty eyes that drink them in.
The motto of the moment, "Show, don't tell."
I take one-fiftieth of a good day's time to say.
"These things," I note, "will make your writing 'good.'"
While in my mind the question lurks, "What words
Of *yours* have graced a page this fortnight past?
You always quote and doers, from their work.
Yet you remain among the 'going to do'
And watch your death approach with nothing done.
Am I the only one," I ask myself
"To pry into these promenades of pomp?"
I vainly search for two, or four, or maybe six
Bright eyes that tell me what no words have dared to say:
"We know you for the hypocrite you are.
You tell us how, and mark our work.
You critic in the artist's marketplace.
We would have done with you, but we have games
To play and grades to earn before you meet our wrath."
But no such rebel cause lies waiting there,
And 'midst the scratch of pencils jotting note
And my too-twangy voice, the end-bell sounds.
I gratefully sigh, "Tomorrow we will write…"
My voice trails off in sounds of shuffling feet.

Time, Time, Time

Alarm clock ringing—
That's the start.
Breaks my sleep,
And breaks my heart.
Finish homework,
Take a shower,
Get my hair right—
Takes an hour.
Hurry, hurry,
Don't be late—
First hour starts
At half past eight.
Catch the school bus,
"Don't be surly,"
Driver's never late
Nor early.
7:50
on the nose.
"Oh my goodness!
There it goes."
Mom'll drive me—
Won't take long—
"Time and Temperature"
Was wrong.
Seven bank clocks
On the way—
None are synchronized
Today.

Coming dates
To ready for
On the marquee
By the door.
"Tempus fugit"
says the sign.
No one's fugits
Fast as mine.
"Bell is ringing—
Gotta go—
I'll be home
With Beth and Joe."

Time, Time, Time—
It's the major reason I'm
Grieving, griping, squawking, whining
In this silly little rhyme.

Open locker,
Grab the books,
Teacher's waiting—
Dirty looks.
Drop the load
Upon the floor,
Just do make it
In the door.
Then the time
Begins
To
Crawl
Trudging
Like the teachers' drawl.

Poke and tarry,
Lag and creep—
Think I'll catch
A little sleep!
Then the end bell
Loudly knells.
(Gosh I hate
to live by bells!)
Hurry, scurry,
Dart and dash,
Hustle, bustle,
Scoot and flash,
Cannot linger,
Cannot play,
My next class
Is blocks away!
Time for pictures,
Time for lunch—
To the lunchroom
With the bunch.
After eating,
It's a tossup—
Time for work
Or time for gossip?
Gossip over,
Duty beckons.
Next hour's bell
Will ring in seconds.

Time, Time, Time—
It's the universe's crime
And I know
If I could ditch it
It would make my life sublime.

Back to classes,
Back to work.
More assignments
Not to shirk.
Chronological
Decisions.
"Due on Tuesday,
With revisions."
"Time to get your
Vaccination."
(Wasn't like this
on vacation!)
School's over—
What a pity!
Now I've got
The float committee.
Saturday we
Wash the cars,
Then we'll sell
The candy bars.
Soccer game tonight
At four—
That'll take an hour
Or more.
Hope they win
The region title.
Then there's Susie's
Dance recital.
Somewhere in there
I'll get dinner.

(Ron MacDonald
makes a winner.)
homework time
at nine or ten.
Tomorrow I will
Try again.

Time, Time, Time—
Life's an uphill,
Dated climb.
And although
I hate to say it,
I'm just sure
I've reached my prime!

DON'T RUSH ME

When Joe was five, he learned to pray
And just before "Amen" he'd say,
"I watched the older boys play ball;
Now is there any way at all
That You could make me eight or nine?
Yes, I think that would be just fine."
And always, without flair or fuss,
God's clear response was always thus:
"Don't rush me, boy, don't rush me."

And so Joe grew from year to year,
But he knew how to persevere.
When adolescence had begun,
He prayed God make him twenty-one.
"Let me forego these teen-age years,
With their anxiety, pain and tears."
But God, whose patience has no bound,
Gave answer in a whispered sound,
"Don't rush me, boy, don't rush me."

When Joe was in the prime of life
He married a lovely, winsome wife.
Their children followed year by year,
And Joe's one prayer was always clear:
"I'm grateful, Lord, for what you send,
But let me see where this will end."
God always knew what Joe would pray,
But he would always wisely say,
"Don't rush me, boy, don't rush me."

Through many smiles and many tears
Joe reached the age of ninety years.
Then God came by and said to Joe,
"You've done it, boy. It's time to go."
Joe smiled and slowly raised his hand.
"Let's not just yet strike up the band.
I've got a little party planned."
And then he asked, without a blush:
    "Besides, Dear God, just what's the rush?"

Southern Memories
(August 1997)

Someday, ages and ages hence,
When white oak leaves turn brown and crisp,
And autumn air snaps cold upon my face,
I'll pull my favorite sweater
Tight around my neck
And savor snapshots
Of that August trip with you.

I'll watch again the hazy rising sun
Through dense Kentucky fog
And sunsets dancing golden
Upon the glassy Gulf.
I'll see us raising glasses high
In seafood restaurants,

And I'll recall those evening swims
In solar heated pools.
And drinking Old Milwaukee
From the cooler red and white
I'll see again you sit cross-legged
On each motel bed,
Trip books and maps spread out
As you prepare
The route we'll take next day

My legs will tingle to the feel
Of warm Atlantic sand,
And through the pounding surf
I'll hear you laugh
At tiny peeps escaping every
White-capped crashing wave.

48

I'll taste again those moving meals
Of peanut butter crackers,
Potato chips and Pepsi.
I'll see Daytona sand upon our tires
And salamanders on the walls
Of that North Line Street house
You once called home.

Our matching broad-brimmed
Black straw hats I'll see,
That sheltered us from baking
Eighth-month sun.

And I'll recall again
The luscious, sensuous memory
Of waking up in eighteenth century
Elegance, plantation style
Beneath a yellow canopy,
Buried in the plushy mattress
Of an antique, large, four-poster bed,
And making love to sounds
Of mocking birds, and wind
Through Spanish moss
On ancient live oak trees.

And I will feel your hand in mine
As we wade knee-deep through the Gulf
Alone at night,
Our murmurs matched by gentle laps
Upon the sandy shore.

Oh, yes, I'll savor snapshots,
To be sure,
But what I'll treasure most
Are all the memories I made with you.

Barges

High on the riverbank of grass,
I watch the plodding traffic pass.

The barges come, the barges go,
Upriver to St. Paul, or so,

Down the river to New Orleans,
With Illinois corn and Illinois beans.

The massive seacraft make their way
Through rain and sunshine, night and day.

Under the bridges and through the locks,
Each barge looks like a giant box.

Thirty-five feet wide, two hundred long,
Their hoppers full, they roll along,

Guided by towboats with river names
Like *John P. Strong* or *Bootsie James*,

Each with a pilot, captain, crew,
And each with a job he has to do.

I raise my arm and pull it down;
The towboat's horn makes a blaring sound.

I think everyone I know
Should watch the barges come and go.

In the Bookstore

I'm sitting in the bookstore,
My favorite place to be.
I'm sitting in the bookstore
With a cup of English tea.
The walls are lined with How-To's,
Romance and History,
But my favorites—every visit—
Are the children's books, you see.
For the world is too much with us—
On that we all agree—
But the "juvenile" authors
Take us where we want to be:
They can put us in a light house,
Or on a ship at sea,
Or in silly situations
Like talking to a tree!
They know that we're still children
As we drink our English tea,
And justify why this is
My favorite place to be.

To Jeannie, On the Night of Her First Symphony Solo

What was it Shakespeare
Called that thing—a "hautboy"?
It matters not,
For writers
When all eloquence
Is finally laid aside,
Are limited to words
Of Aiken, Wilder, Twain,
And led you toward
The primrose Sylvia Plath.
Yet which of these could tell,
In simple words,
Your oboe's lyric strains tonight—
Exquisite, sharp and sweet?
Your liquefacteous pink perfection
In shining lights
Before the silent crowd?
Your mother's radiant, prideful smile?
Or catch the tone in "Absolutely flawless"—
Your music master's double word critique?
The murmuring intermission crowd
Is taken by your "talent,"
And on this score
I have no doubt they're right.
But only pedagogues could know
Your payment price
Of pain and perseverance,

The years of pounding practice,
That brought you to this
Bright and burning hour.
And though I, too,
Like Shakespeare, Plath and Twain,
Am limited to words,
I use them now to say
I feel a teacher's special pride
That I was asked to share
This special night with you.

Grandma's Diary, 1953

Prosaic soul, my grandma
Dedicated to daily entries
Attentive to the weather,
And the health of friends,
She was a rock
Of post-Depression survival.
Housekeeper, loyal to her
Small-down employers,
Concerned about her
Spread-out family,
She was 76 on April 1,
And never told her age.
With no fanfare,
She reported my turning 17,
Graduating high school,
And going off to college.
Not once did she write down
That overworked and
Undervalued "love,'
Yet it was there, on every page.
December 31 she brought
Her cryptic journal to its end.
In hindsight I can add this note:
In three months
She would have a stroke
And spend all her remaining years
Unable to manipulate a pen.

The Substitute

For almost half a century I filled the role
Of "teacher."
I had my place, a room that
I called mine, filled with those artifacts
That make a teacher's "home":
Wall decorations, pictures of
The lions of literature,
A podium, plus
A neat six rows
Of inconvenient seats.
And, at the heart of all of this,
A teacher's chair and wooden desk
Where lay the tools of the trade: a cup of writing
        Instruments,
A stapler, and a roll of tape.

But now—
I am a "substitute," and none of those
Prerequisites that make a house a home
Are mine.
Each day I come
I try to build relationships
And work with lesson plans
Prepared by someone else,
And make sure that, at close of day
The tools are all exactly placed
The way they were
When I walked in the room.

The world is rife with stereotypes
Of hounded substitutes and evil kids
Who make their life a Hell.
But that is not the essence
Of the sadness of a sub.
It really lies
In Tennyson's line:
"O death in life,
The days that are no more."

To Regina

Every single waking hour
Of every single day
A thought of you will cross my mind;
Some pass on by, some stay.

For over 16,000 days
You were a part of me.
Now only memories are left
Of days that used to be.

But Ah! What memories they are!
They buoy my very life,
Which would have been of little worth
Had you not been my wife.

The night Jay Lenne introduced
Us in the Park Bowl bar,
Our wedding day, the honeymoon,
That worn-out Plymouth car.

The Plaza beers, our baby girls,
The moves from place to place,
And I remember, through it all
Your face, your lovely face.

You laughed with me, you cried with me,
You knew me through and through,
And whether you were mad or glad
You told me, "I love you."

Our journey's done—you lie beneath
A stone of granite red.
No longer we'll go hand in hand
Or share our king-sized bed.

But I'll still feel your loving touch
When through our haunts I walk,
And I will hear your voice again
When our girls laugh and talk.

I sometimes cry when I'm alone
And want you hear with me,
But God has better plans for us
Throughout eternity.

So while you help St. Anthony
I'll find some things to do,
And as we wait to meet again,
Remember: I love you.

SONGS

The Little Red Flyer Wagon
(That my Grandpa Gave to Me)

When I was only four or five
My grandpa came one day.
He winked his eye and rubbed my head,
And then I heard him say:
"I've got a big surprise for you
If you will turn around."
I closed my eyes and then turned back,
And this is what I found:

Chorus:
It had white sidewalls and red hubcaps
And "Flyer" written on the side,
And I knew when I saw it
That it wouldn't be long
Before I'd take a ride.
It had a long black handle
And a bed of red
And wheels that spun so free—
That little red flyer wagon
That my Grandpa gave to me!

That wagon brought me so much fun
Throughout my growing years.
I had a lot of laughs on it,
And sometimes even tears.
I'd coast it down the steepest hills,
And one time hit a tree
In that little red flyer wagon
That my Grandpa gave to me (Chorus)

The years went by and Grandpa died,
And I outgrew my toy.
It stood forgotten in the shed
For no one to enjoy.
I've often prayed when times got hard
That God would let me be
Back in that flyer wagon
That my Grandpa gave to me (Chorus)

Now I've got a grandson of my own;
He is my pride and joy.
And I've decided that it's time
For him to have my toy.
I'll sand it down and paint it up,
And then on Christmas Day
He'll dance around and clap his hands,
And this is what he'll say:

(Chorus)
It has white sidewalls and red hubcaps
And "Flyer" written on the side,
And I know when I see it
That it won't be long
Before I'll take a ride.
It has a long black handle
And a bed of red
And wheels that spin so free—
That little red flyer wagon
That my Grandpa gave to me!

Gentleman Farmer

He was over the hill at forty-three,
He was tired of selling stocks, you see,
So he decided he would till the soil.
He had some land full of timber and grass;
He enrolled in a correspondence glass,
And settled in for a life of farmer's toil

Refrain:
He was a gentleman farmer, gentleman farmer,
But he didn't know the first darn thing to do.
He was a gentleman farmer, gentleman farmer,
It wasn't long before his days were through.

He bought some cows and a pair of mules,
Some Leghorn chickens and a lot of tools,
And he plowed some land for a crop of hybrid corn.
He grew some hay in a grassy spot,
And sowed some seeds in a garden plot,
And watched his custom jeans get kind of worn.

Refrain

The crops came in 'bout a half-foot high;
The the summer sun got hot and dry,
And he developed blisters on his feet.
His cows went dry and his dog got mean,
And the sickle broke on his mowing machine,
And his pickup truck expired from engine heat.

Refrain

When it came time to harvest wheat
He didn't have enough to eat,
And the garden didn't yield a single bean.
He began to harbor lots of doubts
'Bout agriculture's ins and outs;
His fattening hogs were looking kind of lean.

Refrain

When winter came he scratched his head,
And thought awhile and then he said
"A man's just gotta find where he belongs."
So he sold whatever things he had,
Bought himself a pen and pad,
And started writing hard-times country songs.

He was a gentleman farmer, gentleman farmer,
But he didn't know the first darn thing to do.
He was a gentleman farmer, gentleman farmer,
It wasn't long before his days were through.

The Monopoly Game
(to the tune of "A Boy Named Sue")

Now the other night I was stayin' home;
My kids were restless and ready to roam,
When one of 'em says, "I know what we can do.
Let's get out the Monopoly set,
And if we tried real hard I bet
We can even get old Dad to join us too."

I looked around for some excuse,
But I knew darn well that it wa'n't no use
They set up that board in record time,
'N my protests weren't worth a dime,
so I just bid my peace of mind adieu.

Now I grew up with that darn game,
And the way it treats me's still a shame.
I never win but I never quit,
And I just know because of it
I look at life with a slanted point of view.

Lady luck is always nice
When I get into a game of dice;
My poker game's just short of great—
I'll even fill an inside straight—
And people think I'm good at roulette too.

But in Monopoly I never fail
To end up goin' straight to jail,
And I'll tell you this: it don't feel grand
Watchin' others buy up land
While you peek through the bars and fret and stew.

Somebody landed on my property,
But I couldn't collect in jail, you see,
Then when I got out I rolled to Chance
And it told me I could just advance
To good old Illinois Avenue.

Well, it wasn't a place where I could dwell;
The kid that owned it had a big hotel!
It took all my cash to pay the rent;
If I wasn't broke, I was kinda bent,
And my attitude began to turn real blue.

Now I don't want to say my kids are mean,
But they aimed to pick the old man clean.
The banker wouldn't give me a loan;
I mortgaged everything I owned
Just to pay a railroad twice the rent he 'as due.

It wasn't long, I'm here to report,
Before I went to bankrupt court,
And I turned my little marker in—I 'as through.
And though it didn't do a lot for me
It sure did help my family;
They all said "Dad, we *like* to play with *you*!"

The Story of the "Emergency Room Blues"

As most of you know, I was attacked by the genus Streptococcus bacteria the Sunday after the February birthday bash in Danville (had a great time, by the way, Debbie and John! Loved having the baptism on Saturday evening—hope Kristin doesn't think it cheapened the event or anything), so I proceeded to miss four days of school, took tons of medicine for ten days (including stuff for 15 fever blisters which broke out on my lips), and figured that would take care of it. WRONG!

Yesterday I told Gina that I still didn't feel well—throat still hurt, no energy, etc. and she insisted that I go to the emergency room at Blessing Hospital. So I take her to work—yes, work on a Sunday, no less—and drove on down. Well, I get in there and I begin to feel like a wuss and I see all these people in wheelchairs, pregnant women, one old lady with a broken ankle, accident victims on stretchers with IVs and everything, but I went on with it. Pretty soon I got in, and the doctor took a culture. Then I proceeded to sit on that stupid table for an hour waiting for the results. I began to wonder what it would be like if ER staff ever got fed up with yuppies in their windsuits trying to get help with their hangnails in the midst of real suffering. And then I got defensive about it, so I grabbed a flow sheet from the box and began to write a blues song (you have to imagine the whang of a guitar chord at the end of each line):

Well, it's 'leven o'clock in the morning'
In the clinic emergency room.
I wait for the doctor to see me
And give me some pills for my gloom.
The nurse checks my pressure and breathing
And puts me in Room 43,
Where I stare at the four walls around me
And wonder what's happenin' to me.
At one thirty in comes the doctor;
He's big and he's gruff and he's mean.
He probes me and sticks me and gags me
Sayin' "Beats all that I've ever seen!"
I've got pregnancies, accidents, punctures,
And head wounds and gout in this session,
And among all this turmoil and wailin'
You've got a store throat and depression?!"

I said:

"No, Doc—I got the BLUES
Clean down to my shoes!
I'm here with the losers,
The victims, the boozers.
But Hey! I got news—
            I still got the BLUES…

        Anyway, you get the picture. Leadbelly is
probably somewhere gagging up his lunch but at least I
wasn't bored. Pretty soon the doctor came in and said,
"Well, the results are positive, so you've still got this
stuff." He prescribed some medicine, and sentenced me
to two days of rest. And here I am, back where I started.

The Gingerbread Boy Rap

Once upon a time way out in the land
Lived a little old woman and a little old man.

They wanted children; they wanted them bad;
But they couldn't have any and they were sad.

Her name was Ellie; his name was Stan,
And they came up with another plan.

One day while Ellie was baking her bread,
She got a big idea in her little old head.

"I'll take this dough I'm working with now
And make a boy--but I'm not sure how."

So she grabbed a bowl of gingerbread dough
And began to roll it really slow.

When she got all finished (it looked like Stan!)
She laid it gently on the bake 'em up pan.

She poured some tea and had some cake,
And waited for the gingerbread boy to bake.

Then she opened the door just a little crack,
And that gingerbread boy came off his back!

He jumped right out and ran to the door,
Through the bake 'em up pans all over the floor.

Ellie said, "Oh, Stan! Our wish came true!
A gingerbread boy and he looks like you!

Oh my goodness! Oh, joy! Oh, joy!
We've got ourselves a gingerbread boy!"

But the gingerbread boy just wouldn't wait;
He was down the steps and out the gate.

They all ran after him--Ellie and Stan,
The little teakettle and the bake 'em up pan.

They shouted "Come back! Our pride and joy!
Our little Pinnochio gingerbread boy!"

But the gingerbread boy kept running away,
Till he saw two men who were working with hay.

He put his gingerbread hands on his gingerbread hips,
And these were the words that came from his lips:

"I outran Ellie and I outran Stan,
I outran the kettle and the bake 'em up pan.

I won't be cute and I won't be coy.
I can beat you too--I'm the gingerbread boy!"

"Well," said the men, "You're a smart little pup.
But we'll catch you and eat you up!

We're Fred and Ferd. Our name's Malloy.
We *know* we can catch a gingerbread boy!"

They ran and ran but they couldn't last--
That gingerbread boy was just too fast.

Pretty soon he stopped and said, "Hey! Wow!
That looks like a big old Guernsey cow!"

He put his gingerbread hands on his gingerbread hips
And these were the words that came from his lips:

"I outran Ellie and I outran Stan,
I outran the kettle and the bake 'em up pan,

I outran Fred and Ferd Malloy.
I can beat you, too--I'm the gingerbread boy!"

"Well, that may be true, little gingerbread boy,
"But I'm the fastest cow in Illinois.

You may beat me, but I don't know how--
'Cause I'm a real fast Guernsey cow!"

She tried to catch him, but she ran too slow.
That gingerbread boy could really go!

He ran so fast and he ran so free--
Till he came to a fox, down by a tree.

He put his gingerbread hands on his gingerbread hips,
And these are the words that came from his lips:

"I outran Ellie and I outran Stan;
I outran the kettle and the bake 'em up pan;

I out ran Fred and Ferd Malloy,
And the fastest cow in Illinois!

They're all after me like a big convoy--
I can beat you too, I'm the gingerbread boy!"

"Well," said the fox, "I'm really impressed.
But this, young man, is not a test.

Now, don't be cute and don't be coy.
I don't want to race you, gingerbread boy.

"We'll trot along together and talk a while.
I've nothing to do for many a mile."

They left the others way behind;
Then they came to a river, and it blew his mind!

The fox licked his lips in foxy style
And then he said, with a wicked smile:

"The river is deep and the river is wide.
You can't get across unless you ride.

"I'll take you over, and I won't fail--
Just grab a seat on my bushy tail!"

Then, half way across, that fox so proud,
Began to howl and cry out loud:

"My tail is sinking! Alas! Alack!
You'll have to ride upon my back!"

They had almost reached the other shore
When the fox began to howl some more:

"My back is aching; I'm almost dead!
You'll have to ride upon my head!"

When the gingerbread boy was on his nose,
Up out of the river that fox arose!

"You outran Ellie and you outran Stan,
"You outran the kettle and the bake 'em up pan;

You outran Fred and Ferd Malloy,
And the fastest cow in Illinois;

You beat them all--I don't know how--
But you can't escape me--I've gotcha now!"

Then he flipped his head, his mouth was wide--
And the gingerbread boy went down inside!

He learned his lesson, but there is no joy--
'Cause *that* was the end of the gingerbread boy!